UP FROM THE ASHES

A STORY ABOUT BUILDING COMMUNITY

By Hannibal B. Johnson

Illustrated by Clay Portis

EAKIN PRESS ◆ Austin, Texas

FIRST EDITION

Copyright © 2000
By Hannibal B. Johnson

Published in the United States of America
By Eakin Press
A Division of Sunbelt Media, Inc.
P.O. Drawer 90159 ⬥ Austin, Texas 78709-0159
email: eakinpub@sig.net
⬛ website: www.eakinpress.com ⬛
Designed by Brian Alexander

ALL RIGHTS RESERVED.

2 3 4 5 6 7 8 9

1-57168-385-2

For CIP information, please access:
www.loc.gov

ACKNOWLEDGMENTS

Special thanks to Donna Berryhill, Cheryl Brown,
Michael Carrasquillo, Cindy Driver, Nancy Feldman,
Sally Frasier, Sarah Theobald-Hall,
Brandon Love, Marvin Love,
Patricia Person and her third–grade class at
Crystal Hill Magnet School in Little Rock, Arkansas,
Brenda Johnson Portis, and Kimberly Tomlin
and her third–grade class at Alamo School in
Galveston, Texas, for their assistance
in reviewing drafts of this work.

My name is James, but everybody calls me Jimmy. I am just a normal nine-year-old kid. I like toys, games, and having fun. I'm a lot like you. I lead a normal life. Well, I used to think I led a normal life. I will let you decide.

My story is about growing up in a place called Greenwood. Greenwood is not a city or town. It's a neighborhood in Tulsa, Oklahoma, where people work together, care about one another, and show each other respect. Best of all, Greenwood is a place where everybody knows my name.

The year I am telling you about is 1921. Warren G. Harding is president of the United States. My state, Oklahoma, joined the Union fourteen years ago, in 1907. My city, Tulsa, became a city twenty-three years ago, in 1898.

Oil was discovered in and around town a few years ago. Some people became wealthy almost overnight. Many others come here every day looking to do the same. Because of all the oil, money, and people, Tulsa has been nicknamed "The Magic City."

People here are divided by skin color. But Mama says that's no different from the way things are in most of the rest of the country.

Things here are all separate. Black people and white people do not live in the same neighborhoods. They don't go to the same schools. They don't eat in the same restaurants. They don't even drink from the same water fountains.

There is one part of town for white people and another part of town for black people. They are separated by the railroad tracks.

Did I tell you that I am black? Well, I am.

Mama says that some black people came here with the Indians. Long ago, many Indians were forced to come here from states like Alabama and Georgia in the south. The journey from the south to Oklahoma was called the "Trail of Tears."

Other black people came here looking for a better life. Some of them found it on Black Wall Street.

Greenwood Avenue is the name of one of our main streets. It's known all across America as "Black Wall Street" because of all the black businesses that are there.

Have you ever heard of Wall Street? That's the fancy street in New York City where people make lots of money. Well, some people probably lose lots of money too. Greenwood Avenue is like Wall Street because they are both busy places.

Black Wall Street is a place where black people provide for their own and do business with one another. I'll tell you a little bit about some of the people and their businesses.

Simon Berry runs a jitney. A jitney is like a taxicab. You can ride anywhere in Greenwood for just a nickel. Mr. Berry also owns a bus company, a special airline for rich oilmen, and the Royal Hotel. Mr. Berry is just one of many successful black businesspeople.

Mabel Little operates the beauty shop that Mama goes to on Saturdays. Mrs. Little's shop

is always filled with the excited chatter of women and girls getting their hair done.

The Williams family runs the Williams Dreamland Theatre, a fancy movie theatre with live entertainment. People come from all around to enjoy the newest movies and the best of our local musicians.

J. B. Stradford is a well-known attorney and businessman who owns the Stradford Hotel. He makes lots of money.

Barney Cleaver is our first black policeman. He patrols the Greenwood area.

B. C. Franklin has a law office. He is a lawyer for many people, even some who cannot afford to pay him.

Arthur C. Jackson is a respected doctor who

performs operations. He is so good at what he does that he is known all over the nation.

In Greenwood there are newspapers, grocery stores, theaters, clothing stores, beauty shops, cleaners, hotels, doctors' and lawyers' offices, and more. We've got everything here. Greenwood is even becoming a center of jazz music. You've heard of jazz, haven't you? It's a mix of gospel and blues music that many people say began in New Orleans, Louisiana.

Mama and Daddy take me and my sister, Jean, to the Williams Dreamland Theatre in Deep Greenwood almost once a week. Deep Greenwood is where Greenwood Avenue and Archer Street meet. It's the most lively corner in Greenwood.

I love sitting in the dark, munching on hot buttered popcorn, sipping a pop, and watching the latest movie. That's why the Williams

Dreamland Theatre is my favorite business in Greenwood.

Anytime you go to Deep Greenwood, you will see beautiful, proud people. But there's something special about Thursday nights. Thursday is maid's day off. Many black women do housework in the homes of rich white people. When they are off from work on Thursday nights, they all come down to Greenwood to relax and have a good time.

Mama says that with their faces all painted and dressed in their Sunday best, the ladies look like fashion models on a Paris runway.

With all the bright lights, noisy cars, and excited people on Greenwood Avenue, I sometimes think I'm on that famous street in New York City called Broadway. I'm not sure what Broadway is like, but it must be something like Greenwood—a bundle of sights, sounds,

smells, and full of happy people. Just being there always brings a smile to my face.

In Greenwood, we have everything that they have in the white part of town, and maybe more. Mama says that Greenwood has a spirit and a soul all its own.

Like I said, my life is normal. Well, it was until May 31, 1921. That is when the problems between black people and white people got out of hand. Mama told me the whole story of how the trouble started.

A nineteen-year-old boy named Dick Rowland bumped into a seventeen-year-old girl named Sarah Page in an elevator downtown on May 30, 1921. Dick is black. He's a shoeshine boy. Sarah is white. She's an elevator operator.

I know Dick, but not Sarah. Dick is my friend. He's like the big brother I always wanted. He

looks out for me and gives me spare change—just a few pennies every now and then. He's even teaching me the shoeshine business.

Dick got on the elevator so he could go to the third floor in the Drexel Building in downtown Tulsa to use the restroom. That is the only restroom that Dick can use because he is black.

When Dick got on the elevator and the door closed, the elevator jerked. Dick bumped into Sarah, who was operating the elevator that day. She screamed. A clerk from a nearby store ran to help Sarah. Dick was scared, so he ran away.

Before long, rumors began to spread. People were saying that Dick had attacked Sarah in that elevator. That was not true.

The police arrested Dick and took him to the jail inside the courthouse downtown. He was locked up in a cell on the top floor.

Sarah later told the police that Dick had accidentally bumped into her on the elevator. But by the time she spoke up, it was too late.

The next afternoon, one of the local newspapers came out with a big story saying that Dick had attacked Sarah in the elevator. Shortly after the story appeared, a large white mob formed down by the courthouse. Many of them had guns. They were angry. They wanted to punish Dick for what they thought he had done to Sarah.

The black men in Greenwood began hearing about what had happened to Dick. They knew his life was in danger. They promised one another that they would protect Dick.

Dozens of black men, many of them with guns, assembled in Greenwood and walked down to the courthouse. Sheriff McCullough met them on the courthouse steps. He told

them to go back home. He said that he had things under control.

Sheriff McCullough told the black men that he had taken Dick up to the top floor of the courthouse. He said he had shut off the elevator so that no one could get to Dick. The black men were satisfied that the sheriff was doing all that he could to protect Dick, so they started back home.

Meanwhile, the large group of white men who had gathered at the courthouse grew even larger. The black men, worried about Dick's safety, returned to the courthouse.

At the courthouse, the two groups were yelling and calling one another bad names. Then somebody fired a shot. That's how the Tulsa Race Riot of 1921 started.

The riot began on May 31, 1921, and ended the

next day. By the time it was over, Greenwood was raided by hundreds of white men. They burned it to the ground. The homes, the businesses, and even the trees went up in a cloud of thick, black smoke. The fires lit up the night sky like it was the Fourth of July.

Bullets flew. Bombs dropped. Glass broke. It didn't seem real, but it was.

I thought the whole world was on fire. I soon discovered that only my world was. Greenwood was burning. Our churches, homes, and businesses all went up in bright red flames and thick, black smoke.

During the riot, the mob went on a rampage, destroying everything in sight. Mama says that the men in the mob were blinded by hate.

We live next door to the church we attend on Sundays. It's called the Mount Zion Church. The mob broke into our house. The first thing

the mob did was set fire to our curtains. We were lucky. Mama saw the men coming and hid my big sister, Jean, and me under her bed. I was so scared that my whole body shook. I said The Lord's Prayer over and over in my head.

The men in the mob took some of our best things, like our dishes, silverware, and jewelry. They broke most of what they didn't take. Then they left.

When she thought it was safe, Mama came and got Jean and me from under the bed. I was still shaking. I ran into the living room and peeked out the window. I couldn't believe what I saw through the breaks in the thick, black smoke.

Women in their nightgowns, holding the hands of their little children, were running down the railroad tracks. They were dragging their children along. The kids were crying.

I guess they were running down the tracks to keep out of the mud. Mama said that they must have been trying to get away from the riot. But she said that she thought there was nowhere to run.

Our house was still standing after the riot. We were able to put out the fire in the house ourselves before it got out of control. Daddy's business, a popular roller skating rink on Greenwood, was totally destroyed. He hasn't been the same since. Still, Mama says that we are fortunate because we did not lose the most important thing—each other.

By the time it was over, almost all of Greenwood, Black Wall Street, was gone. It hurt me to see all the places I love turned into nothing but ashes. I cried when I found out that my favorite place, the Williams Dreamland Theatre, was gone. Mama says that no one can ever take away my memories, though.

I wondered where Daddy was all this time. Mama told us that Daddy and other black men were captured. Like prisoners, they were told to hold their hands high above their heads. They were marched through what was left of Greenwood to the Tulsa Fairgrounds, the Convention Hall, and McNulty Baseball Park. The black men were told that they were being held in these camps so that they would not be harmed by the angry white mob. They were told that it was for their own protection. Daddy wound up at the Tulsa Fairgrounds.

The women and children were left alone in Greenwood. Even though Jean and I were with Mama, we were so frightened. I tried so hard not to cry, but I couldn't keep the tears from falling.

After two days, Daddy was released. Those were the longest two days of my life. Our family was reunited.

Governor Robertson called in the state troops and declared martial law. I didn't know what "martial law" was, so I asked Mama. She said that "martial law" means that military troops take over and run the city.

The troops told us where we could go and where we could not go. They told us what we could do and what we could not do. But by the time the troops came in and took over, all the damage had already been done.

Tulsa was put under a "curfew." Mama says a "curfew" is just like a special rule. It tells you when you can do certain things, like when you can be on the streets and when you can open your business. I already knew what a "curfew" was because I have one. Well, my bedtime is nine o'clock. I think that's a curfew!

The curfew was for people who were free. But

most black men were not free. They were in the holding camps around town. No one could get out unless he had a green card signed by his boss.

When it was all over, Greenwood looked like a battlefield. Hundreds of people had been killed for no reason. Even more people were hurt. Many people lost their homes and businesses. Everybody lost something.

After the riot, the Red Cross helped us with food, shelter, and clothing, but many of our friends and neighbors spent months living in tents through the cold, hard winter and the hot, steamy summer.

I don't think I've ever been so sad in all my life. I wondered how people could be so mean to one another. Mama said, "Nobody is born that way. Hate has to be taught."

I asked Mama how we would make it through all this. Mama said, "Greenwood is a community, and a community comes back, even in the worst of times."

We started rebuilding even before the fires went out. We haven't stopped yet. We don't have much money, but we still have one another. Everybody in Greenwood pitches in to help everybody else. It's hard work, but I know that we will come back bigger and better than ever.

When my church, Mount Zion, was burned to the ground, it was only six weeks old. My Sunday school class has to meet in the church basement or in somebody's house. Last Sunday, we met in Mabel Little's house.

Our minister, Reverend Whitaker, tells us to have faith. Faith, he says, is when you believe

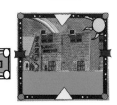

in something with all your heart and soul. Even though we no longer have a building, Reverend Whitaker says that we are still a church. He says it's the people that matter, not the building.

I do have faith. Every time I see Simon Berry strolling proudly down the street, or catch a cheerful wink and nod from Mabel Little, or see Barney Cleaver's mile-wide smile, I have faith. I know that it's the people that make Greenwood beautiful.

Like I told you from the start, my story is the story of Greenwood. I hope that you live in a place like Greenwood—a place where people help one another in good times and bad, a place where people respect one another, a place where everybody knows your name. Mama says that's what community is all about.

AN UPDATE ON
THE GREENWOOD COMMUNITY

This book is based on a true story. Greenwood is the traditional African-American community in Tulsa, Oklahoma. Greenwood is also the name of the best-known street in the community.

Greenwood's reputation throughout the nation as "Black Wall Street" came about because of the successful black-owned and black-operated businesses there. The Tulsa Race Riot of 1921 destroyed all that, but the people of Greenwood refused to give up. The community was rebuilt and came back bigger and better than ever. It peaked in the 1940s. At one time, there were 242 businesses in Greenwood.

With the end of segregation and changing economic and social conditions, Greenwood began to decline in the late 1960s and throughout the 1970s. Greenwood now stands ready for another rebirth. The Greenwood Cultural Center is its centerpiece. In the coming years, Greenwood is expected to become a leading arts and entertainment center for the Tulsa community.